Ooey-Gooey Animals

Earthworms

Lola M. Schaefer

Heinemann Library

Chicago, Illinois

Customer Service 888-454-2279
Visit our website at www.heinemannlibrary.com

Designed by Suzanne Emerson/Heinemann Library and Ginkgo Creative, Inc.
Printed and bound in the U.S.A. by Lake Book

06 05 04 03 02
10 9 8 7 6 5 4 3 2 1

Library of Congress Cataloging-in-Publication Data
Schaefer, Lola M., 1950-
   Earthworms / Lola Schaefer.
      p. cm. — (Ooey-gooey animals)
Includes index.
Summary: Provides a basic introduction to earthworms, including their habitat,
diet, and physical features.
   ISBN 1-58810-504-0 (HC), 1-58810-713-2 (Pbk.)
   1. Earthworms—Juvenile literature. [1. Earthworms. 2. Worms.] I. Title.
   QL391.A6 S327 2002
   592'.64—dc21

                                        2001003026

Acknowledgments
The author and publishers are grateful to the following for permission to reproduce copyright material:
Title page, pp. 8, 11 E. R. Degginger/Color Pic, Inc.; p. 4 David Liebman; pp. 5, 7, 14, 15, 16, 18, 20, 21, 22 Dwight Kuhn; p. 6 Steve Callahan/Visuals Unlimited; p. 9 Science Pictures Limited/Corbis; pp. 10, 12 Rick Wetherbee; p. 13 Bruce Davidson/Animals Animals; p. 17 Arthur R. Hill/Visuals Unlimited; p. 19 David June

Cover photograph courtesy of David Liebman

Special thanks to our advisory panel for their help in the preparation of this book:

Eileen Day, Preschool Teacher
Chicago, IL

Paula Fischer, K–1 Teacher
Indianapolis, IN

Sandra Gilbert,
Library Media Specialist
Houston, TX

Angela Leeper,
Educational Consultant
North Carolina Department
of Public Instruction
Raleigh, NC

Pam McDonald,
Reading Teacher
Winter Springs, FL

Melinda Murphy,
Library Media Specialist
Houston, TX

Helen Rosenberg, MLS
Chicago, IL

Anna Marie Varakin,
Reading Instructor
Western Maryland College

Some words are shown in bold, **like this.**
You can find them in the picture glossary on page 23.

Contents

What Are Earthworms?

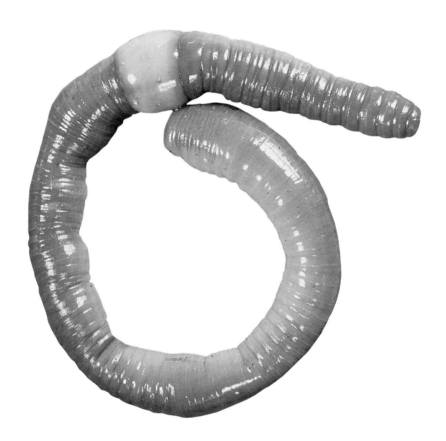

Earthworms are animals without bones.

They are **invertebrates**.

mouth

Earthworms are long and thin.

They have mouths.

Where Do Earthworms Live?

Earthworms live in the ground.

Their homes are called **burrows**.

burrow

Earthworms spend most of the time in their burrows.

They dig deep into the ground when it is cold.

What Do Earthworms Look Like?

Young earthworms are white.

Adult earthworms are dark colors, like brown.

rings

Earthworm bodies are shaped
like tubes.

Their bodies are made up of more
than 100 **rings.**

What Do Earthworms Feel Like?

Earthworms feel gooey.

Mucus covers the skin of their bodies.

mucus

Mucus helps earthworms slide through the dirt.

How Big Are Earthworms?

Earthworms can be as short as your finger.

Some earthworms are longer than a table.

This earthworm is as almost as wide as a man's finger.

How Do Earthworms Move?

Earthworms crawl on and in the ground.

They wiggle and push their bodies along.

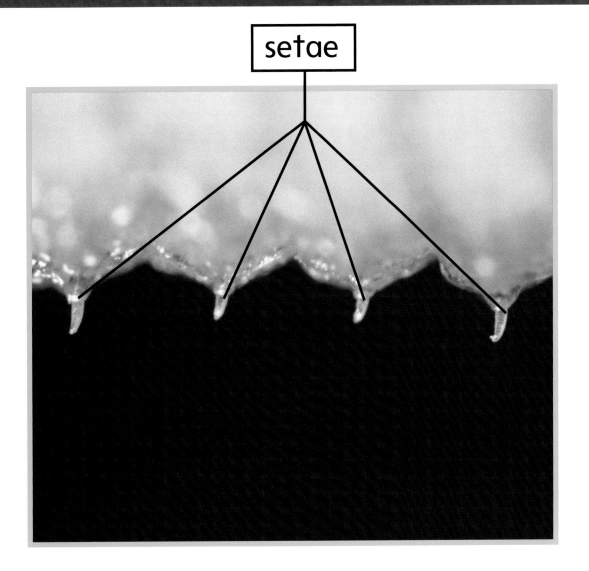

setae

Strong hairs help them hold on to the dirt.

The hairs are called **setae**.

What Do Earthworms Eat?

Earthworms eat dead plants.

They eat seeds, roots, leaves, and stems.

As earthworms dig, they eat dirt.

Sometimes they eat a bug or two.

Can Earthworms Help People?

Earthworms are good for farms and gardens.

They mix up the dirt as they dig.

People use earthworms to catch fish, too.

Where Do New Earthworms Come From?

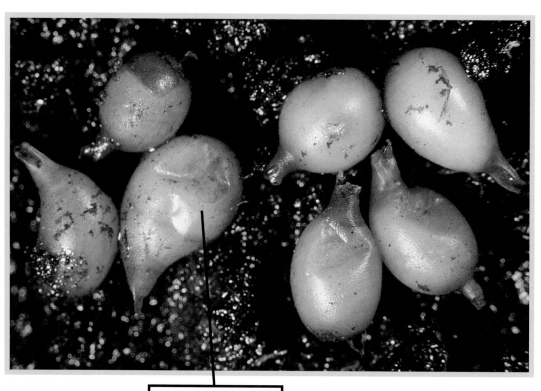

cocoon

Adult earthworms use their **mucus** to make a **cocoon**.

A cocoon is a safe place to lay eggs.

The eggs hatch.

Little earthworms come out.

Quiz

What are these earthworm parts?

Can you find them in the book?

Look for the answers on page 24.

?   ?

Picture Glossary

burrow
pages 6, 7

mucus
(MYOO-kus)
pages 10, 11,
20

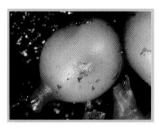
cocoon
(kuh-KOON)
page 20

ring
page 9

invertebrate
(in-VUR-tuh-brate)
page 4

setae
(SEE-tee)
page 15

23

Note to Parents and Teachers

Reading for information is an important part of a child's literacy development. Learning begins with a question about something. Help children think of themselves as investigators and researchers by encouraging their questions about the world around them. Each chapter in this book begins with a question. Read the question together. Look at the pictures. Talk about what you think the answer might be. Then read the text to find out if your predictions were correct. Think of other questions you could ask about the topic, and discuss where you might find the answers. Assist children in using the picture glossary and the index to practice new vocabulary and research skills.

! CAUTION: Remind children that it is not a good idea to handle wild animals. Children should wash their hands with soap and water after they touch any animal.

Index

Answers to quiz on page 22

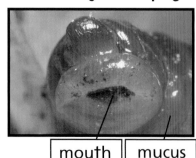

mouth | mucus